The
Cocktail
Competition
Handbook

The Cocktail Competition Handbook

BY ANDY IVES

Mixellany

All correspondence should be addressed to the publisher's attention at: Mixellany Limited, The White House, Nettleton, Chippenham SN14 7NS United Kingdom.

Text design by Mixellany Limited

Cover design by Ivana Mijalkovici

Author photo, page 111: Wendy Pereira

First edition

British Library Cataloguing in Publication Data Available

Softcover: ISBN: 978-1-907434-50-1

Contents

Preface

The first competitions I judged, some fifteen years ago, were won by bartenders who employed daring new techniques, like using fresh fruit juice or setting something on fire. In those early competition days, it was easy to come up with an approach no-one had seen before. Good chat would often carry a bad drink. And if you screwed up, the only people to know about it were ones who saw it happen with their own eyes.

Those were the cocktail competition's Wild West days. Things are very different now. Brands have adopted competitions as their favourite way to engage with bartenders, and corporate sponsorship has brought with it prizes that range from desirable to life-changing. Winning the right competition can now advance a bartender's career by leaps and bounds, sometimes bringing worldwide exposure that extends beyond the bar industry and out into the real world.

As competition prizes have evolved, so has what is required to win them. In this book I describe what I believe it takes to consistently win cocktail competitions in the modern bar industry, which requires of competitors not just creative presentations and tasty drinks, but also an understanding of sponsor brands' values and an awareness of the role the press and social media play in the judging process.

Whether you are just embarking on a competition career or count yourself an old hand, I hope these observations, which have been gleaned from experience gained by judging hundreds of heats over the past fifteen years, will help you win more of the competitions you enter and get as much as possible out of the cocktail competition as a whole.

NB. In this book:

Pirates = boring trivia tangentially related to alcohol

Aardvark = home-made cocktail ingredients, 'artisanal' spirits

PART ONE

Preparing for a Competition

"Measure twice, cut once."—Carpenter's proverb

Johnny Bartender awakes.

He cracks open one gummy eye and surveys the crepuscular scene, finding himself to be in his own bed and alone. Surprised and annoyed by the latter, he turns his attention inward and conducts a battle-damage assessment: moderate kidney-burn; severe hollow-stomach; negligible head-thump; and categorises his hangover as a three-out-of-ten: not worth worrying about. Half way through a mental inventory of the contents of his fridge, he remembers: Today is his day off.

Good intentions flood through Johnny Bartender; thoughts of alcohol abstinence, clean food and exercise. 'That's it' he says out loud. 'I'm going to the gym.'

One hour later, Johnny is sitting at a bar, nursing a Red Snapper he wishes he had made himself. While he waits for Jenny Bartender to arrive, so that they can 'go and have a quick look at the place that just opened down the road', he takes out his phone and navigates to BarLifeUK.com, wondering if those lazy douchebags Simon and Andy have posted any-

thing ranty about the latest Spirited Awards an-
nouncement. Nothing. 'They are losing their edge,'
says Johnny.

Moving to the 'Competitions' page, he sees three
new ones: corporate vodka, flavour-of-the-month
rum, and tasty-but-obscure gin.

'Hmmm,' thinks Johnny, twisting one waxed end of
his ridiculous moustache, 'It's been a while since I
did a comp.'

CHAPTER 1
Choosing the Right Competition

COMPETITION TYPES

Cocktail competition season—which in the UK generally starts in April and tails off towards October—sees scores of comps take place all over the country. The different sponsor brands and competition formats can make it seem as if the variety of competitions is endless, but in actual fact they all fall into one of six categories:

- Local, bartender organised
- Local, brand organised
- National, brand organised, one-off
- National, brand organised, annual
- Global, brand organised, one-off
- Global, brand organised, annual

At first glance, it might seem as if there isn't much to be learned from this. In reality, understanding the differences between these competitions—who will be judging them and, crucially, what sponsor brands will be looking for in each case—can help set you out on the right path should you decide to enter one. This is especially important for bartenders just starting their competition career, as picking the wrong debut competition can lead to a dispiriting experience likely to put them off comps for life.

LOCAL COMPETITIONS

Local comps are the bartender equivalent of a band playing pub gigs: It is here you learn how competitions work at a fundamental level and, perhaps most importantly, how you will deal with performance anxiety, before going on to play the big stages.

Bartender-organised local comps tend to be fun, sometimes messy affairs. The prize will usually be a bottle of something that won't make it as far the winner's home, and the judges will be 'local heroes' of some stripe: senior bartenders or managers, possibly a local press hack who won't know what they are doing. Good chat is often well rewarded, and as no sponsor brand is involved, there won't be a strict brief. In other words, you are expected to get up there, smash out a good drink and be entertaining. Funnily enough, as loose as bartender-organised local comps can sometimes be, 'smashing out a good drink and being entertaining' goes a fair way towards winning something like Bacardi Legacy, so as you can see, the foundation skills for a competition career can be found here.

Brand-organised local comps are one rung up the sensible ladder. And with that comes the need to spare at least some thought to the needs of a sponsor. Typically, small, local comps will hosted and judged by the brand's regional rep, so you won't have to be too concerned about upsetting a PR department by dropping an F-Bomb during your presentation. However, the rep is going to want to justify the budget being spent with some social media photos to post, so lines of caster-sugar cocaine garnish are not going to win you any prizes. And, as this is a brand comp albeit a small one, there will be a brief to follow and some brand knowledge to impart if you are to win. These last two elements—sometimes missing from bartender-led comps—are vital skills to master as you work your way up the competition ladder.

The best thing about both types of local comp is that there is no life-changing prize at stake, so the pressure is off. You are free to experiment, get any public speaking jitters under control, and begin to learn how to best express yourself to an audience and panel of judges. While there are no negative repercussions for losing, winning local comps can start to build a bartender's reputation, and give them the confidence to enter bigger comps in the knowledge they have already got a handle on the basics, and know they can present in the spotlight without soiling themselves.

NATIONAL COMPETITIONS

The key component of national competitions is the heat final format, meaning a number of regional qualifying heats will be held around the country with the winners going through to a national final.

Things are starting to get quite serious at this level for three reasons: firstly, there will be much more press coverage of a national comp. Secondly, the prizes get bigger, often a trip to an overseas distillery, or a decent wedge of cash. Thirdly, the brand is spending a lot of money on the competition, and they will want some return on this investment.

Quite often, sponsor brands will offer some form of part-time ambassadorship to the winner of a national comp. For bartenders who see an expense account and first-class lounges in their future, this can be a leg up towards the great ambassador gig in the sky.

However, even if the comp does not offer this as a prize and even if you have no interest in becoming a brand ambassador, be aware that every national competition sponsor will be viewing potential winners through a PR lens. At some stage, the brand manager will have a meeting with their boss, who will ask 'So how did the competition go? How did you spend my £10,000?' At this stage, showing the big cheese a photo of an obviously hammered bartender, receiving a layback while wearing a 'You're All Cocks' t-shirt won't fly. In other words, if you want to win a national comp, you need to take it somewhat seriously.

As the 'serious' level increases at a national comp so does the 'learning from and bonding with your peers' element. Most national comps hold just three or four heats in major cities, meaning bartenders often have to travel to take part. Even if the heat is in your city, you will be up against out-of-towners. This is really where a bartender can start to expand his or her competition chops. As great a foundation as local, community-organised comps are, they are a bit like playing pool with your best mate: there's only so much to be learned from going up against the same person over and again. The potential for learning increases yet again should you make it to the final, where you will ostensibly be up against a group of the best bartenders the country has to offer. Win or lose, you will learn a shit load.

The entry mechanic for a national comp requires careful consideration. A major brand offering a decent prize can receive hundreds of entries. This list will be whittled down to forty or fifty regional competitors. Generally, you will be asked to submit your cocktail specs and some sort of supporting statement. This could be a description of how you created the recipe or an explanation of your inspiration. Either way, it needs to be lucid and well written. Don't forget, you are being viewed through a PR lens. Omitting information or horrendous spelling and grammar are your enemies. Don't flush the time you spent creating a drink down the toilet for the sake of using spell check or getting a friend to read your text and make sure it makes sense, before submitting it.

GLOBAL COMPETITIONS

In format, global comps are no different to national comps. There will be regional heats, leading to a national final. But things don't end there: the winner of the national final will go on to compete against other national winners in a global final.

Obvious examples of global competitions are Bacardi Legacy and World Class. Winning the UK final of one of these can be career-defining; winning a global final can be genuinely life changing, so it should come as no surprise that the serious levels are off the charts.

There is a particular state of mind required to win one of these big, global comps. It is best described as 'assuming a role', rather than simply entering a competition. Sponsor brands spend hundreds of thousands of dollars on these competitions, which form the cornerstone of their trade marketing strategies. A half decent drink served in your grandma's teacup won't cut the mustard. To win Legacy or World Class or any other global comp, the brand needs to see you as the epitome of its values. This sounds nebulous, and frankly, a bit pretentious, but it is nonetheless true. From the moment you submit your entry, the competition needs to seep into your working and social-media life.

Essentially, you need to live the comp for the months leading up to it and breath the sponsor brand. This might seem like a lot of effort for a cocktail competition at first glance, maybe even intrusive. If you feel this way, it could be that global comps aren't for you. However, if you follow any of the previous Legacy and World Class winners on Facebook and covet their lives, be prepared to go all-in when you yourself enter.

Adherence to the competition brief is absolutely key to global comps. Your drink will need to not only taste good, but also perform as an 'ambassador cocktail' for the brand all over the world. Think very carefully before including complex, homemade ingredients or super-exotic, hard-to-source components. Simplicity and ease of replication tend to do well in global comps.

Global comps have long run times, especially if you progress past your regional heat and can take up several months of your life. This is worth discussing with your employer before the comp kicks off. Get all the dates straight in your head before booking holidays, weddings or other 'can't move' plans. Winning a regional heat, but pulling out of the national final because you forgot you booked a week in Magaluf makes you look like a dumbass.

CHAPTER 2
Finding Inspiration

Inventing a new cocktail, writing a song, or painting a portrait all have one thing in common: they are expressions of creativity driven by some form of inspiration.

The word 'inspiration' conjures a mental image of clouds parting and a beam of sunlight descending to illuminate the lucky artist. We imagine it to be a big, grand, driving force. In real life, inspiration can be as mundane as thinking 'I wonder what would happen if I did this'. Or in cocktail terms it can mean saying 'I wonder how this would taste with that'. The father of the thought might be unremarkable, but the resulting 'new thing' can be game-changing.

Competition drink inspiration is likely to come from one of three areas:

•   The sponsor brand's liquid
•   The sponsor brand's story
•   An element of the competition brief.

Lets call the first area 'drink first' and the second two areas 'presentation first'.

DRINK FIRST

This is probably the most straightforward approach to take. Finding inspiration in the liquid inherently means the drink is your first priority. With a close eye on the competition rules, you can experiment and revise until the recipe is perfect. With that nailed, you can then turn your attention to the 'chat' element of the brief and create a presentation that wraps brand knowledge, the thinking behind your drink, and something of your personality around your cocktail.

Because the 'Drink First' approach mirrors what you do every day—flavour matching, experimenting, having fun with booze—it will more than likely result in a tasty, well balanced cocktail. However, bear in mind that many of your fellow competitors will be following the same process, especially if the competition brief pushes entries in a particular direction by way of a theme or ingredient limitations. Now is the time to listen to every 'Hmm, this is weird, but I wonder' thought that pops into your head, in an effort to come up with a drink sufficiently novel to stand out from the rest of the field. In other words, don't play it safe.

PRESENTATION FIRST

While the 'Presentation First' approach often results in an entertaining performance, it can also make perfecting the drink more difficult as it imposes an additional set of limitations on the bartender. Competitors who are inspired by a concept often latch on to a physical, historical or geographical property of the brand story. For instance, a brand could be based in one country but import its raw materials from somewhere else. Creating a cocktail with ingredients solely originating from those two places is a sound concept.

However it does immediately limit the tools at your disposal, especially when combined with whatever general rules the competition imposes.

The key to the 'Presentation First' approach can be summed up as 'don't neglect the drink'. In other words, in being inspired to explore a concept, you may come up with the best, most interesting and engaging presentation ever seen by the judges. But if the drink tastes like crap, you won't win the competition.

KILL YOUR DARLINGS

'Kill your darlings' is a literary term. It describes the situation in which an author realises a piece of writing that he or she is particularly pleased with is holding back the story as a whole. Despite loving that paragraph or character, the author is forced to remove it for the greater good of the novel. Behind waffle-induced time penalties, reluctance to kill darlings is the most common cause of competition failure. To illustrate, here is an example:

> The creator of Aardvark Gin loved the apple trees growing outside her distillery so much, she made them the logo for her brand.
>
> Johnny Bartender's mum has an apple tree in her back garden. So Johnny gets the train across the UK to go scrumping at the family home, only to find the fruit doesn't taste very nice. Scrapping the idea of a muddled apple foundation, he decides instead to make apple jam. The first batch tastes incredibly bitter, so he makes a second batch, adding loads of sugar. This ruins the balance of his drink, so he experiments with adding various bitters and vermouths, until finally he runs out of time, and is forced to say

'Oh well, that'll do.'

At the competition, Johnny delivers a moving presentation about his relationship with his Mum, and
the story of Aardvark Gin's founder. However, his
cocktail induces in the judges a vomiting fit not
seen since the film Stand By Me. And although impressed by his performance, they score him in last
place. Johnny goes home disappointed and annoyed
that he expended so much time and effort for nothing, and resolves to never enter another cocktail
competition.

Johnny was so invested in using apples from his mum's garden as
a concept that he missed all the signs telling him the drink wasn't
going to work. We see bartenders make this mistake at competitions all the time. The telltale signal is a recipe which contains
multiple small measures of modifier such as half a bar spoon of
bitters, 2.5mm of vermouth, and a dash of absinthe. This level of mi-
cro-tuning of balance can (but not always) point to a fundamental
problem with the recipe, often caused by sticking with a concept
that doesn't work.

So, if you feel inspired to explore a concept with your competition
entry, don't do so to the detriment of the drink. In other words, if
you can't get the recipe to work, kill your darlings and start again.

ACTION POINTS

•   Whether inspired by the base spirit or the brand's story, the
drink must work

•   Don't allow commitment to an idea blind you to a flawed
recipe

- It is better to have a great drink and a mediocre story, than a thrilling presentation and a rubbish cocktail. However ideally, both should be top-notch.

CHAPTER 3
The Drink

LOOKS GOOD, SMELLS GOOD, TASTES GOOD.

A good drink is the throbbing heart of a cocktail competition entry. It needs to be balanced, delicious, sufficiently different to existing recipes that it can be considered original. And it must look appealing, too. Even within the confines of a competition's rules, the number of possible ingredient combinations and avenues to explore is infinite. So where the hell do you start?

I am not remotely qualified to answer that question because I am not a bartender. And even if I were, I'm not sure there is ever a single 'right way' to tackle a creative process. However, a cocktail competition book that does not look at this subject would be incomplete. So to provide an example of one approach to this conundrum, I turned to someone who—for my money—is one of the best all-round competition bartenders in the UK.

Chelsie Bailey, one of Bristol's finest, has won every competition heat in which I have been a judge. She is the 2016 Chivas Masters UK Champion, and before that, Chelsie won the Appleton Estate Bartender Challenge. As described elsewhere in this book, it takes more than a just good drink to win a major competition, and Chelsie has mastered the art of wrapping good chat around her cocktail. However, leaving brand knowledge and storytelling aside for the moment, I spent some time talking to Chelsie about her approach to creating a competition drink.

AI: Tell me about your first-ever competition.

CB: My first comp was a Chartreuse National one. I think it was in 2011. That was when I first moved to Bristol. I made (laughs) a Chartreuse Key West Cooler (laughs) that I definitely tried to layer.

AI: How long had you been bartending at that point?

CB: At that point, it must have been about a month.

AI: How did the Key West Cooler turn out?

CB: The bottom layer was Green Chartreuse, mint, and then the middle layer was Yellow Chartreuse with ginger and lemongrass cordial, and then the top was the Chartreuse Cassis with cayenne pepper in it (laughs).

AI: Did the drink work?

CB: Absolutely not. Every time that picture pops up on my timeline, I giggle at myself. (Laughs) It was awful.

AI: So that was competition number one. And you didn't win. What was it that made you want to enter more, even though you lost?

CB: The one thing I got out of that comp was how much I researched Chartreuse, because if I hadn't entered that comp, I wouldn't have ever gone into that much depth about its flavour. I kept trying it and trying different things.

AI: Looking back, you know now the drink didn't work. But at the time, did you know?

CB: No, not at all.

AI: So you tasted it, but didn't know it was bad. It's not that the process you went through was broken. It was that your palate wasn't educated enough at that point to know whether it worked or not?

CB: Exactly. And when I practiced, it layered every time. But at the comp it didn't layer. When you stirred it all together it didn't taste particularly bad, but the colour was awful.

I've related this part of the interview for a couple of reasons. Firstly, it is a perfect illustration that everyone has to start somewhere. If gambling on cocktail competitions were a thing, I would never bet against present-day Chelsie Bailey. And yet her competition chops aren't innate. When she first started out, she—just like most competition rookies—sucked. For anyone reading this book in preparation for their first competition, don't be discouraged if you crash and burn. It's all part of the process.

My second reason for including this passage is what Chelsie was doing as she answered my questions. Sitting on the table in front of her was a stack of hard-back notebooks in which she had recorded all of her competition experiences. She was able to turn to the pages relating to the Chartreuse competition and show me the specs as she wrote them in 2011. There were similar entries for every other competition she has entered. I am convinced that this approach, of recording everything and never losing a scrap of information or forgetting a lesson learned, dramatically speeds up the process of going from rookie to major competition winner. It links all of the competitions together, and instead of existing as isolated events, they become a cumulative learning experience.

We then went on to talk about the 'middle period' of Chelsie's competition career, during which she gained more experience and trained her palate. For the sake of brevity, I won't relate the entire conversation. But in summary, she described a number of competitions in which she got the drink concept right but its execution was wrong or vice-versa. The picture she painted was of a person finding and perfecting her process. The interview resumes below, at the point we begin to discuss the method Chelsie now uses to create competition drinks.

AI: Tell me about the first comp you won.

CB: (Asahi Rising Stars regional heat) ...This is when I began using the principle of using three or four ingredients. All my competitions now, I try and base them on the principal of four ingredients—liquor, sugar, water, bitter, and then add stuff to it if I want to. I am about to enter the Tahona Society competition that has a brief of tequila, sustainability and Mexican street food. I said to myself 'let the flavours go, and think about the brief'. Everything that came up—sweetcorn juice, citrus, Tabasco—everything I wrote down, I then said 'nope, that's not what I am doing'. Let's do something that you wouldn't normally associate doing with Tequila.

AI: To say that concisely, let all of the obvious ideas come into your head, then kick them out.

Would that be a fair representation of what you are describing?

CB: Yes, pretty much. You need to think outside the box. For me, if I think 'I'm definitely using this ingredient', it will get stuck in my head and I'll end up adding a load of ingredients to it and it won't work... Instead, I looked at the sustainability angle and thought leftovers, 'what do we always have lots of left over at our bar' and it is egg yolk. So let's do a Tequila Fizz.

Chelsie then goes on to describe the rest of the recipe, which I will omit for the sake of space. We jump back in, having talked about the other ingredients she will use in her Tahona Society cocktail.

AI: How do you arrive at the final spec? Do you try something, find it doesn't work and leave it for a few days, waiting for a new idea to pop into your head? Or is it more methodical?

CB: Sometimes it is methodical, sometimes I completely blag it (laughs).

AI: How much of the process is tasting something and deciding what should be added to it, and how much of it is conceptual? How much of it is 'mental tasting' for want of a better term?

CB: The majority of it is conceptual. For example, I know a Tequila Fizz is going to taste banging. I know that Tequila, tonic, egg yolk is going to go together. So then it is 'how do I make it more interesting'. And at that point you start playing with flavours to modify it... Sometimes it's about kicking ideas out of your head by a process of elimination.

AI: That competition, which has the brief of Tequila, sustainability, and street food, is quite constraining. It is leading you down a certain path. How would you approach a comp with no rules, that just says 'make a drink with this spirit'?

CB: I would get the [brand's] website up and sip the drink... The best example would be the Mount Gay comp. I sipped Black Barrel and looked at the website. You see how they want the brand to be portrayed... This gives me a target. Imagine I'm sipping Chivas. I might think 'hmm, I'll make a Pina Colada twist with this', if I'm not looking at the website (Chelsie makes a gesture that suggests straightening a knotted tie). It keeps my ideas on the straight and narrow.

AI: So for both types of comp, you need to have something spark your imagination. There are infinite combinations and possibilities, and you need to find a way of triggering your brain to say 'go that way'.

CB: Yes, I just need to have that one starting line that allows me to create a theory for the drink and go that way with it.

AI: So the foundation of your technique is to find a way of narrowing down the options.

CB: Yes, I sip the spirit and I put myself in a situation, whether that is in relation to the brief or how they want the brand to come across, or if, for instance, the prize is a trip to Barbados, I ask myself, how would I want to drink this rum if I am sat in that situation.

AI: So what you are doing there is putting the spirit in a context. Once you have an idea of the context, that is when you think about the 'four ingredient' principle. Is it fair to say you would start simple, and then start a process of additions and substitutions to get the drink to work?

CB: Yes, if I want it to be a stirred drink, I'd start with the spirit, a sweetener and a bitter. And if it's a shaken drink I'll start with the spirit, something sour and something sweet to balance it... After fine tuning it, I then decide how I'm going to serve it. What glass? What garnish? Does it need ice? Then I'll leave it for a few days and try it again because sometimes I think you can convince yourself you like a drink. But with fresh eyes you either think it still works, or needs something else.

Following the interview with Chelsie, I have come to the conclusion that her competition success is due in large part to the following three things:

Meticulous record keeping: Chelsie has recorded every aspect of her competition career, from day one. Every recipe variation is written down along with feedback from judges as well as notes on what worked and what didn't. Her notebooks are full of knowledge to which she constantly refers, meaning that mistakes are generally made just the once. And successful ways of working are identified and used again.

Identifying context: The time that Chelsie spends at the beginning of the creation process—sipping the base spirit and immersing herself in both the competition brief and the brand's story—gives the flavours she is experiencing context. This means that any ideas which subsequently pop into her head are generally heading in the right direction. And perhaps most importantly, her process of 'mental tasting' and 'conceptual exploring' happens in line with the competition brief. It seems to me that this approach helps cut down the variables, and reduces the number of false starts she makes.

Foundation principle: Chelsie's 'four ingredient principle' means that once the context or concept of the drink is straight in her head, she knows how to begin to express it in liquid terms. Instead of a scattergun approach, Chelsie's methodology is almost scientific.

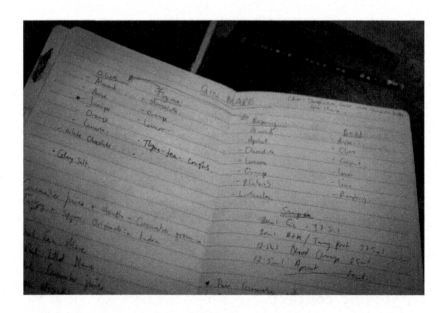

She is always starting from the same point, getting the basic flavour right, and then fine-tuning by way of adding modifiers, or substituting ingredients.

A similar approach may or may not work for you. As I've said several times in this book, there is no single 'right way' to create something new be it a piece or art or a cocktail. However, if there is one thing that every bartender who hopes to win more competitions should take from Chelsie's example it is record keeping. The only real way to get better at something is to practice it and learn from both successes and failures. If you do not write newly-gained knowledge down and continually refer back to it, there is a danger it will slip away, dooming you to repeat the same mistakes over and again. This process of cumulative learning also means there is no such thing as a bad entry, every drink you create adds to your store of knowledge, and by those terms, has value whether or not it wins a competition.

WHAT'S IN A NAME?

'What's in a Name?' was the first thing to pop into my head when it came to titling this section on competition drink names. It was also the first thing to pop into the head of anyone who has ever written about naming anything. Thus, you've heard it before. It is boring at best, corny at worst, and displays a lack of imagination. The same can be said of at least half the cocktail names you see at the average competition heat. Given that the name of your cocktail will be scored, usually accounting for around 10 percent of your total marks, a rubbish name can be the difference between winning and losing a close heat.

Naming competition drinks should not be approached in the same way as naming drinks for your regular menu. The latter need to be descriptive, yet evocative. The ideal response to reading it would be 'Ooh, that sounds nice'. Competition drink names aren't there to make a customer salivate. Their job is to tie the various elements of your presentation together: The explanation of your inspiration, demonstration of product knowledge, and choice of ingredients should all be reflected in the name you choose for your cocktail. It doesn't necessarily need to sound tasty. But it must encapsulate everything you have said and done while making the drink for the judges.

GO DEEPER

These days, brands are very keen to talk about history: when and where they were founded; how long they've been around; their connections to socio-economic history. Reading about this stuff will often turn up the inspiration for the formulation of your cocktail and its name. However—and this is a big however—when you go about this, don't skim the surface. Everyone in the comp has access to the same information as you and will likely find similar things within it interesting. Don't latch on to the first thing that grabs your attention. Dig deeper. Find tangents. Go off on them. Drop the first few ideas that come to you, because they will have come to everyone else, too. Find an angle that is uniquely yours. Take both the inspiration for the drink and its name from that. And then laugh your ass off when, at the heat, three bartenders have all given their drinks the same name and everybody else's presentation is about pirates.

GLOBAL PICTURE

Everything in the previous paragraph goes out the window when it comes to big, global comps like Bacardi Legacy and World Class. The cocktails that win such competitions go on to become part of the sponsor brand's history. They feature on menus and in cocktail books for years to come. As such, descriptive elements become less important (the name will always be used in the context of the brand so you don't need to allude to what is in the drink). An evocative, imagination-capturing name becomes the way to go. This is an esoteric process. It is difficult to describe how best to go about it other than to say you will know a good name when you hear it. You are essentially inventing a new consumer brand. You should chose a name accordingly. Look to the brand's past for inspiration, obviously, but also look to perfume and couture brands for ideas. It may seem crazy, but drinks that win global competitions are marketed in the same was as these FMCG [fast-moving consumer goods] products.

ROAD TEST IT

Cocktail names are like haircuts, sometimes it takes another person to tell you that yours is shit. Whatever type of competition you are entering, test the name (and drink) on as many people as possible, ideally a mix of colleagues and punters. Laughter is a bad sign, as is the lack of comprehension. Should you keep needing to explain the name, take the hint and change it. Don't get so invested in a cocktail name that you stick with it, despite evidence that other people don't get it (See the section on Killing Your Darlings).

ACTION POINTS

• It is dangerous to come up with the name at the beginning of the process, this can lead you down dead ends and tie you to a broken foundation idea

• A good competition name should tie all elements of your presentation together

• A global competition drink name should look right on the side of a bus

CHAPTER 4
The Presentation

SAY WHAT?

The words you say as you make your cocktail will account for half of your marks. This is true whether you are taking part in a small, locally-organised contest or the grand final of a global competition. Thus, it makes sense to put just as much effort into to your verbal presentation as you do your drink.

There is of course no single 'right way' to go about this just as is there is no right way to create a cocktail recipe. But there are good presentations and bad ones. By examining the differences between these, it is possible to identify some areas of 'good practice' that can start you off on the right course.

UNDERSTAND WHAT THE JUDGES SEEK

There are three broad topics that your presentation needs to cover:

1. The concept behind your cocktail

2. A display of brand knowledge

3. Your bartending personality

Cocktail Concept: This is an explanation of why you have cho-

sen a particular set of ingredients and what you intend the judges
to experience as they drink it. Once your cocktail spec is finalised,
this should be fairly clear to you. However what remains to be decided is how you will communicate it. At the very beginning of the
presentation-creation process, simply write down a version of this
explanation in as few words as possible. This paragraph will serve as
a summary of the 'cocktail concept' information you need to work
into your pitch.

Brand Knowledge: A method for determining what brand
knowledge needs to be shared is described later on in this chapter.
Once you have completed the process it describes, you will end up
with several brand facts or themes that need to be communicated.
Write these down in summary form as you did with your cocktail
concept.

Bartending Personality: This is potentially both the most
difficult thing to pin down, and also the most engaging part of your
presentation. Your bartending personality is the part of your way
of working that remains unchanged, regardless of the bar you are
behind. For example, you could pull a shift at The American Bar at
the Savoy, and dress, speak and serve in one way, and the next night,
do a stint at Trailer Happiness, dressing and serving in a completely
different manner. And yet you would be the same bartender with
the same interests, preferences and passions. Perhaps a better way
of describing this is to think of Jimi Hendrix playing rock, blues, and
funk. It doesn't matter what genre of song comes on the radio,
you know Jimi by the way he plays. In this example, years of being
influenced by other guitarists and playing with different musicians
produced Jimi Hendrix's unique style, and it is no different for a
bartender. Identifying your style—or bartending personality—gives

you a constant place to work from when creating competition presentations, and can help you be effective no matter the variety of
spirit or type of comp you enter. Again, find a way of summarising
this, whether it be a paragraph description or simply a list of words
or phrases that you think describes what you are about.

At the end of this process, you end up with three chunks of information that need to be integrated and expanded until they become a five-minute narrative that flows around the physical act

of making a drink, while at the same time being entertaining and informative. A good way to do this can be found at the heart of one of humankind's oldest activities—storytelling.

STORYTELLING TECHNIQUES

'The dustmen woke me up this morning, at six fucking ay-em. Times like that, this country's gun laws make sense. If there'd been a tool under my pillow, I'd have gone on a rampage. But I live in Tooting, not Texas, so I did what English people do and bottled up the fury while I made a cup of tea. I could still hear them, slamming biffa bins around and talking bollocks about football, as I emptied the kettle of last night's dregs and filled it with freshly drawn water. I noticed a distinct anger-tremor in my hand when I dropped the teabag into a clean, china mug. PG Tips, none of that English Breakfast nonsense, and the mug had thin walls, because my Mum maintains that keeps the tea hotter for longer. I don't know. Anyway, I poured the boiling water in and left it to brew for a minute, and turned on the radio. Fucking adverts, of course. They were still blaring when I took the bag out and poured in a splash of semi-skimmed, enough to make the right shade of brown. Pantone 153C if you want to be picky. Gave it a quick stir, and raised the mug to my lips. Just starting to relax, when the news came on. Fucking bin men striking for more pay. I almost choked.'

People often describe storytelling as the process of taking a reader or listener on a journey. This is absolutely true of course, but storytelling is also the art of delivering important information by means of entertainment. As you will have no doubt observed, the previous paragraph, which I wrote in the style of Martin Amis' character John Self, contains quite precise tea-making instructions. Imagine a cocktail competition, during which nine people woodenly recite recipe specs and brand facts, and one person weaves the same information into a story which entertains the judges, and it's easy to predict which competitor will nail the 'chat' scoring category. This is why storytelling, or building a narrative, is just as important as a tasty, well-balanced drink, when it comes to winning comps.

BEGINNING, MIDDLE, END

Stories famously consist of a beginning, middle, and end. The beginning sets the scene and introduces the characters in their starting situation, often describing who they are, and where they are from.

During the middle part of the story, sometimes referred to as the story's crisis, something will happen to dramatically change the characters' situation, forcing them to adapt in order to overcome obstacles and challenges. The end of the story, or its resolution, is all about the characters' new reality. More often than not, the message is one of transformation, how the characters have changed as a result of their passage through the middle part, or crucible, of the story.

This three-phase structure has obvious synergy with making a cocktail:

- Phase one, introduce and measure the ingredients
- Phase two, combine the ingredients (shake, stir, throw etc.)
- Phase three, garnish and serve.

In the same way a story's characters change as they progress through an adventure, so too do the ingredients of a drink, once they are combined, chilled, diluted, and otherwise transmogrified at the bartender's hands.

In other words, every time you make a cocktail, you are telling a classically structured story:

> I took these things, smashed them all together, and now they are this other, new thing.

As you write your presentation, keep this three-phase structure in mind. Your hands are already doing it, so come up with a presentation that fills the five minutes you have behind the bar with words that do the same.

FACT OR FICTION

It's important to note that telling a story within your presentation does not necessarily mean creating a work of fiction or fantastic tale. Rather, it is the practice of creating a five minute narrative that flows and has structure.

This could be as simple as identifying three or four main points you need to get across, then figuring out things to say that fill the gaps and move the presentation smoothly along, in tandem with the various actions of making a drink. In other words, know what you want to be saying about each ingredient as you pour it, what you will be saying as you shake, and at every point in between until you serve the cocktail to the judges. This sounds obvious, but a great many bartenders say 'I'll wing it' when it comes to the linking portions of their chat, and their presentations often stutter as a result.

However, the best competition bartenders go a step further, taking those important points and weaving them into a story that describes events and journeys experienced by themselves, and their ingredients:

Example 1: 'I travelled here, tasted this and experienced that, and as a result, my drink has turned out like this.'

Example 2: 'I used to work here, and learned this. Then I worked there and learned that. Now I work here, and tasted this for the first time, and as a result, my drink has turned out like this.'

Example 3: 'Historically, this ingredient was used like this. I decided to try using it like this instead, in combination with that, because the base spirit is from here, where they produce this and that. As a result, my drink turned out like this.'

Or any number of variations along similar lines, all of which are preferable to: 'The base spirit has peach and aardvark notes, so I added some peach bitters and aardvark hair. The distillery opened in 1947. *Long silence while shaking* Then it burned down in 1959. *Long silence while flaming dried aardvark scales over the glass* Here's my drink. It's called The Peachvaark Martini.'

BE YOURSELF

By its very nature, the bar industry attracts gregarious characters who find holding court and public speaking easy. But that does not mean it is necessary to be a motormouth-Robin Williams clone in order to be a good bartender. Far from it, in fact. Some of the best bartenders are studious types who prefer to practice their art in the background, quietly revolutionising the industry by way of geekish obsession with spirits and experimentation with equipment that borders on the scientific.

If you are of the latter mould, or any other stripe of bartender that doesn't conform to the 'big chat' stereotype for that matter, do not feel the need to be anything other than yourself in order to win a competition.

For a start, artificial big-chat-banter often comes across as fake or cringeworthy when employed by a person to whom it does not come naturally. Secondly, a natural raconteur will beat you at this game. Thirdly—and most importantly—one of your goals at a competition is to stand out from the rest of the field. Making the judges lean forward with interest—as opposed to leaning back and out of the way of wildly gesticulating hands—makes you memorable. At the end of the comp, as the judges add up the points and confer about the result, they will all say 'that studious bartender really knew his/her stuff'. And the brand judge will reply, 'yeah, you could put them in front of anyone without worrying they'd say something stupid'. Such exchanges regularly decide close heats.

STRUCTURE AND TIMEKEEPING

It is always the bartenders who pace and waffle for two minutes before touching a bottle that go overtime in competitions. Using storytelling techniques to create a three-act structure for your presentation—and linking this to the physical act of making the drink—will automatically lift you ahead of half the field before the judges have tasted a drop.

Viewing your presentation as a three-act performance can also prevent mistakes. When you link what you say to specific parts of the drink-making process, you become less likely to ramble and go overtime. Also, with enough practice, synchronising your words and hands can prevent missed-ingredient cockups: If you find yourself at the end of Act One with your hands and words out of sync, it's a safe bet you forgot to put something in the drink, which you can then fix before going on to Act Two.

The bigger the competition, the more important this skill becomes. At the very top level, it moves from important to vital. It is impossible to win a competition like World Class or Bacardi Legacy without having a fully-formed, brand-tailored story for your entry, not just to be told on stage as you compete but to accompany the cocktail as it goes out into the world and becomes part of the sponsor brand's history.

ACTION POINTS

•   Identify a few important points you need to convey, then create a narrative that links them together
•   Break your presentation down into three 'acts', and practice linking your words to specific drink-making actions
•   Telling a story that entertains the judges will always score higher than a recited list of facts and dates

BRAND KNOWLEDGE

Imagine the following scenario: Someone you have met once or twice secretly thinks you are lovely and wants to put bits of you inside bits of them. So the person does some light Facebook stalking and finds out you are into Eagles of Death Metal. The next time you are both in the same room, the person nervously approaches. And while staring you intensely in the eye, he or she recites the date the band was formed, names of the members and their dates of birth, plus its entire discography. Unless this person is really, really hot, you probably won't put out.

Same scenario, same person. But this time he or she casually engages you in a relaxed conversation about music, steering it towards Eagles of Death Metal. When you say 'Ooh, I like them', they say 'Hey, I've got tickets to see them tonight, wanna come?', and you say 'I'd love to!' and then you have lots of sex, buy a puppy together and post a really fucking annoying number of photographs of it on Facebook.

For everyone other than your Facebook friends, the second scenario produces better results, and the process is exactly the same with brand knowledge in comps.

On average, half of the competitors in a heat will spend two out of five minutes pacing behind the bar, reciting the history of the brand in exactly the same way the three previous competitors did. Not only is the person wasting time that could be better spent making their entry drink to a high standard, he or she doesn't stand out from the crowd.

Instead, you should emulate the suitor in scenario two and sift through all the information available about the brand, identify a killer angle, and weave it into the fabric of your presentation so that it underpins everything else you say and do during your presentation.

WHY IS THIS IMPORTANT?

On paper, the way you demonstrate knowledge of the sponsor brand will account for about 20% of your marks. In practice, it's more complicated.

The standard heat judging panel will consist of two independents, often a journalist and a previous winner of the comp, plus someone from the brand. The independents will be much less concerned about the brand knowledge category (predominantly because they don't know much of it themselves) than, say, how the drink tastes, and are likely to score it generously. Drop a few pertinent dates and something about production methods, and you will get high marks from them.

However, the brand judge will have a much closer eye on this category. If at the end of the competition things are tied, or very close, it is this facet of the presentations that will cause he or she to come down on one side or the other. At a regional heat, with a panel of two independents and one sponsor, this is less of an issue. However, should you progress to the later stages of a competition, especially a global one, you will find that the panel changes with more people affiliated with the brand acting as judges. It is at this point that the importance of the brand knowledge category grows exponentially.

With this in mind, it is fair to say that the brand knowledge category is both overtly important, and has a subtext:

Overt importance: It accounts for 20% of your marks, and can make the difference between winning and losing in a close heat.

Subtext: Sponsor brands sometimes place more significance on this category than the marks attributed to it might suggest.

STAY ON TARGET

In scenario two, the suitor achieved a good result because he or she learned the object of affection liked Eagles of Death Metal, so the person researched the band and found one key piece of information: It was playing a show that night.

It is exactly the same with competitions. A hour spent on Wikipedia and the brand's website will provide you with an enormous amount of information. It is then up to you to decide what you need to focus on. But how do you do this?

In some cases, it will be overtly stated in the competition brief. For example, a brief might say 'create a drink inspired by the terroir of our vineyards'. In this instance, you can forget about history, and find a way to concentrate on geography and flavour that no one else considered.

If the brief is vague, or if it has thrown the onus back on you by saying 'express yourself' in some way or other, you need to look a little deeper to identify what the brand is interested in at this moment in time. Good places to start would be trade magazines and websites: Have any stories been written about marketing campaigns the brand has recently launched, or new products, or personnel that have been hired.

If this approach doesn't yield any clues, speak to the brand reps and ambassador. Ask what projects he or she is working on, and what bartenders are being told in the person's training sessions.

The point of this is: To win consistently, you need to go the extra mile. Don't just recite a list of facts and figures like the sweaty stalker in scenario one. Find a killer angle, and weave it into your presentation like the puppy-lover in scenario two.

BRAND KNOWLEDGE AND RECIPE INSPIRATION

This subject is examined in greater detail in the chapter on inspiration, but it is fitting to mention it here, too. The inspiration for your recipe will probably come from one of three areas:

* Something about the liquid
* Something about the brand
* Something about your life experiences

If you find that inspiration for your drink comes from the sponsor brand's history, be very conscious of not veering away on weird tangents that end up delivering no substantial brand knowledge.

At BarLifeUK, we call this 'Pirate Syndrome'. If we had a pound for every time we have judged a bartender who believed he or she was delivering a presentation about a Caribbean rum but who in actual fact talked about pirates for five minutes, we could afford to pay for our own drinks at The Artesian.

ACTION POINTS

* Don't recite a list of facts and figures, that's what everyone else will do
* Look to the trade press and brand staff for clues at to what the brand is interested in right now
* Once you have found your killer angle, weave it into the fabric of your presentation
* Don't go off on weird tangents

CHAPTER 5
Self Promotion

NO, I WON'T VOTE FOR YOU

Competitions sometimes require entrants to promote their cocktail. This generally happens during the latter stages of a comp, when the field has been narrowed by regional heats or some sort of paper judging, and takes one of two forms: Vote for Me, or, The Marketing Plan.

VOTE FOR ME

'Vote for Me competitions suck' said any bartender working at a small bar in a quiet suburban town. And they would be right because this style of self-promotion is easier for competitors who work in busy, city bars, and have lots of industry mates. The suburban bartender might have a fantastic drink—by far the best in the field—yet they stand very little chance of beating a popular, well-known city competitor with a mediocre cocktail, simply because it is difficult for them to collect enough votes.

Vote for Me competitions are also quite cynical on the part of the sponsor brand. The 'vote for my drink' mechanic is employed purely to generate lots of social media posts for the sponsor. It adds nothing to the quality of the competition and the bartenders who enter gain nothing from it.

All of that being said, this type of competition is here to stay. And for any number of reasons, you may decide to enter one. If so, you will no doubt turn to social media in order to promote your cocktail.

Make it engaging: Your competition entry is sitting on a sponsor brand's website. The brand has given you a link, which you will now post on Facebook, asking for votes. The first thing to bear in mind is that in the entire history of cocktail competitions and Facebook, no-one has ever seen a 'Heyyyy guys, pleeeeease vote for my cocktail, I reallly want to win and go to Mexico:) !!!' post made by some unknown person and thought: 'Hmm. I think I will click that link, read their spec and make the drink. Then I'll make all the other drinks and see which one I like best, and vote for it.'

If you post something like this, the only people who will cast a vote in your favour are those who actually know and like you—along with anyone who thinks you look foxy in your profile picture. To get strangers to cast a vote, you need to find a more engaging way of presenting your entry. For example, consider making up a batch of your drink and spending a night off going from bar-to-bar, speaking to any bartenders you don't know, and getting them to taste your drink. Once you have formed this connection with as many people as possible, then post your 'vote for me' link.

As with many things suggested in this book, finding a way to engage with voters requires an investment of time and effort that might seem daunting, but it is a willingness to take these little above-and-beyond steps that consistent winners all seem to have in common.

Try not to alienate your audience: If you post a voting link to your Facebook timeline and then in any industry groups you belong to, all in one sitting, everyone who is 'friends' with you and a member of the same groups will see your post multiple times. This will irritate 'in real life' friends, and actively piss off random Facebook acquaintances. I myself have shouted 'No I will not fucking vote for you' at my computer screen several times in such circumstances. And while this may seem like a trivial concern, a single vote lost because you irritated a friend could cost you the comp.

It is far better to drip-feed these posts, preferably changing the message slightly each time. Done this way, anyone who sees your post multiple times is repeatedly and unobtrusively reminded to vote as the competition deadline approaches. Rather than slapping everyone in the face and telling them to vote five times on the first day, you get to slap them in the face once a day for five days, which allows you to maintain promotion throughout the length of the competition, with less risk of alienating your constituency.

THE MARKETING PLAN

Any bartender with designs on a brand job, or the desire to one day open a bar, can learn valuable skills while taking part in this kind of competition. As opposed to the 'vote for me' mechanic, which tends to devolve into a one dimensional popularity contest, 'marketing plan' competitions force competitors to look outside of their established social media networks, and engage with the industry as a whole.

This type of competition generally gives competitors a defined period of time in which to promote their cocktail to bars and consumers, and is judged on a whole range of metrics, such as press coverage, sales increases, and creativity of ideas—all things that brand personnel and bar owners need to be good at in order to succeed.

Bacardi Legacy is probably the best example of a marketing plan comp, as it provides its late-stage competitors with budget to spend on events and support from ambassadors throughout the process, ranging from the inception of marketing ideas to rolling out the plan and making it work. A global mega-comp like Legacy is not going to be everybody's cup of tea. But increasingly, smaller national competitions are adopting elements of the marketing plan approach. Thus any comp that offers an ambassadorship as its prize is a likely candidate.

Marketing Plan competitions are superior to Vote for Me competitions principally because they create a symbiotic relationship between brand and bartender: The brand gets exposure and the bartender learns skills that will be useful throughout his or her career. However, these competitions can seem daunting to anyone who has lived the kind of blessed life that has not previously required the them to think in marketing terms. In such cases, these steps can help to provide a place to start devising your plan:

Understand your objectives: The scope of potential events and activities open to you will obviously depend on the amount of budget you have been given (if any) and the metrics against which you will be judged. As an extreme example, a global comp might hand you a couple of grand and say 'go for it'. At this point, your mind will race and your imagination fill with visions of all the cool shit you can do with that money. However, before you blow the lot on a jacuzzi limo tour around Tales of the Cocktail, take time to understand exactly what it is you are being asked to do.

Some of your goals are bound to be specific and tangible: Get your cocktail listed in as many bars as possible, for instance, or generate as much trade and consumer press coverage as possible.

Other goals could be more nebulous, such as 'throw the coolest bartender event of the year', or 'get people to talk about your cocktail'. As you progress through the process of writing your marketing plan, the best way to tackle these esoteric challenges will become clearer. However, at the outset your main task is to spot opportunities that hit several birds with one stone. For example, you could send out a load of samples of your cocktail to journalists in the hope they will write about it, which is a good idea in isolation. But, if you know you are going to throw a party, it might be preferable to save the budget that posting samples would use, and invite the journalists to the bash instead.

Keep sight of your original inspiration: The marketing plan element of a competition generally starts once you get past regional heats and are in the running for a place in the final. It is important to keep the inspiration or story of the drink that got you this far in mind when creating concepts for your plan. The events you host and the press you generate should support your cocktail by having their roots in the same inspiration. It isn't enough to get lots of people to come to a party. They—including any journalists who will write about it—need to clearly see the event as an extension of the thinking behind your cocktail's concept.

PR agencies are your friend: This works whether or not you have been given a marketing budget. The sponsor brand will have a PR agency, which has been retained in order to generate press coverage for their client. To this end, PR agents are always looking for (yet seldom finding) not-shit things to put in the press releases they churn out for journalists. Find out who the competition sponsor's PR agency is and build a relationship. Let the agency know about any events you host. Tell the company each time a new bar lists your drink. There is a very good chance the agency will begin to incorporate your competition news into the brand's press releases. All it takes to access this resource is a couple of phone calls and a little initiative.

Engage with the trade press: The first thought to enter a trade journalist's mind as they switch on their computer is 'how can I write about this thing in a slightly different way to the previous 150 times I have written about it'. Consequently, if you phone one and say 'would you like to cover the fifteen tasting sessions of my cocktail I have scheduled around the country?' you will likely get a lacklustre response. However, if you call and say 'I'm doing a load of tasting events around the country. Would you be interested in an article about the different bartending scenes in the cities I visit?' the journalist will probably take your hand off.

Trade publications are always looking for interesting industry content and it is highly likely that you will be able to create some during your campaign. If you aren't sure what a trade publication might constitute as interesting, give them a buzz and ask. Also, don't be concerned about your writing skills or any lack thereof. If you are going to provide a journalist with an interesting story, the person will almost certainly be happy to help you knock it into shape.

This is another of those instances in which a couple of phone calls and a bit of thought can generate press coverage that will count a great deal towards your marketing targets And it will be totally free of charge.

ACTION POINTS

- The competition sponsor's PR agency can be a valuable ally
- Build a relationship with the trade press, find angles that will make them more likely to cover your cocktail
- Imagine yourself being exposed to your own social media posts, and moderate accordingly

PART TWO
Competition Day

"You're afraid of the audience, aren't you?"

"Yes, but it's not stagefright. It's that I'm there as the geek. They like to watch me eat my shit. But it pays the light bill and takes me to the racetrack. I don't have any excuses about why I do it."

—Charles Bukowski, Women, 1978

It's closing time.

As Johnny Bartender slides the deadbolt shut, he can see the last regular to leave standing outside, swaying gently in the breeze as he waits for an Uber.

Now that the shift is over and all the customers gone, Johnny's mind is free of distraction and his thoughts turn to tomorrow's comp. A flush of apprehension flutters in his stomach, but he also feels something else: A light yet insistent pressure on each shoulder.

He turns his head to the left, and a scarlet-skinned, black-horned demon, about six inches tall, looks back at him. From behind its back, Satan's spawn produces a bottle of Tequila. It leans in close, and Johnny feels hot breath on his ear. 'Lets have a drink," The demon says. 'One won't hurt.'

Just then, Johnny feels a small hand gently grasp his chin and turn his head towards his right shoulder. There stands a tiny, yet perfectly formed, angelic version of his mum. 'Now now, Johnny,' His mini-mother says. 'Big day tomorrow. A clear head catches the most worms.'

'That doesn't even make sense,' Johnny is about to say. But the angel and demon have disappeared, scared away by the loud beep emitting from his phone.

Johnny looks down at the screen. It is a message from Jenny Bartender.

'We're at the Ruptured Spleen, having a nightcap. There's a Boilermaker waiting for you,'

CHAPTER 6
Competition Etiquette

DO UNTO OTHERS AS YOU WOULD HAVE THEM DO TO YOU

It's competition day. You have woken up hangover-free after a good night's sleep and successfully navigated public transport incompetence as well as traffic jams to arrive at the competition venue with time to spare. Once inside, you see a sleepy bartender setting up the bar, a collection of nervous-looking competitors clustered in quietly-chatting groups, and some brand folk trying to get a pop-up sign to stay erect long enough for a few photos. Having taken in the scene, what do you do next?

Well, now would be the wrong time to look in your bag and check you packed everything you need, yet at least one competitor will do exactly this, and realise the batch of aardvark syrup the person made last night is still at home in the the fridge. Don't be this person.

Everything else you need to do in between arrival and performance is either an extension of your preparation or simple courtesy. This stuff falls squarely under the banner of 'common sense' and will come naturally to most bartenders. However, nerves and performance anxiety can make even the most rudimentary information fall out of your head. So the following reminders may prove useful.

PREPARATION

Ingredients, ice, glassware and storage: Depending on the situation, you may use various bits of kit and ingredients supplied by the host bar. Introduce yourself to venue staff and check that everything you need is on hand. If you have brought ingredients that need refrigeration or require access to the venue's kitchen, now is the time to sort this out.

Running order requests: Introduce yourself to the competition organiser, so the person knows you are present and can stop worrying about the growing list of no-shows. If you are rostered to work later that day and need to leave before the competition ends, now is the time to ask for an early slot on the running order.

Get the lay of the land: Spend a few minutes behind the bar. Figure out where everything is. If you are using a blender or anything else that needs power, check that there is an accessible socket. If you are using the bar's juices or syrups, now is a good time to taste them so that you are mentally prepared for things to be sweeter or more sour than you usually use. Generally get your head around the space.

COURTESY

Mingle: Introduce yourself to the other competitors. Getting to know your fellow bartenders and learning different approaches to competitions will make the experience valuable, regardless of whether you win or lose. Say hello to the judges. See if you can discern any clues about each person's 'judging type' that will allow you to tweak your delivery and score extra points.

Respect your fellow competitors: It is infuriating when spectators fail to shut the hell up while a bartender is performing. By all means have a laugh with your fellow competitors, but as soon as someone steps behind the bar, keep quiet and listen to what the person has to say just as you would want him or her to do for you.

Accept the result with good grace: If you feel like you should have won but didn't, grit your teeth and congratulate the winner. Have a chat with the judges. Ask for feedback (as described later in this book). Nine times out of ten, you won't feel too bad about losing and it won't be hard to swallow a defeat. However, on very rare occasions, you might feel genuinely hard done by. This could be because you think the winner didn't obey the rules or that you have been marked down unfairly. Whatever the reason, ask one of the judges for a private chat. Explain your grievance. It's unlikely the result will change, but you will get any concerns out in the open. You may well end up seeing things from a different and potentially useful point of view at the end of the discussion. Either way, it is better than having a public, angry row that makes you look like a sore loser.

Don't be a no-show douchebag: This obviously relates to your conduct before the competition, but still falls under the courtesy heading. If you cannot make it to the competition, for whatever reason, let the organisers know. From a personal perspective, in relation to the competitions that BarLifeUK organises, I don't mind if you call or email to cancel the night before the comp. I don't mind if you cancel an hour before the comp. But if you simply don't turn up, you will always and forever be a douchebag in my mind. You may not give two shits about my impression of you: a point of view I can respect. But the other judges and competition organisers will think you are a douchebag, too. And one day, you might want to ask one of them for a job. You may well forget that competition no-show, but they won't.

CHAPTER 7
Bar Craft

THE FINE ART OF AVOIDING FUCK-UPS.

I once attended a Tales of the Cocktail seminar hosted by Stanislav Vadrna, in which he likened bar craft to wiping one's backside after a bowel movement. The point he laboured to make is that repetition can bring grace to physical movements. While this is true, the real lesson learned by all in attendance is to never again pay money to watch Stanislav Vadrna speak about anything.

Back in the real world, there are two elements to good competition bar craft. The first has the mundane function of ensuring you don't fuck up and lose easy points. This applies to everyone. The second relates to bar craft as performance. This can be used or ignored depending on your bartending style.

There are several ways your bar craft can cost you points. The first relates to prejudices that might be held by the judges. The second concerns mishaps and accidents.

AVOIDING THE JUDGES'S PREJUDICES

The best way to avoid the judges' prejudices is to assume the worst of them. Imagine each member of the panel to be a nightmare combination of UKBG arm-garter enforcer and public health inspector. The person might not be. One or two judges may have even worked a bar shift or two. But the safest route is to perform as if at least one judge will deduct points for anything perceived to be unhygienic or 'improper'.

For example:

Handling ice: If your hands are clean, I don't care if you touch the ice that goes into my drink. Some judges strongly disagree and will deduct points if you touch the ice or garnish with bare skin. Whatever your thoughts on this subject, during a competition the safe approach is to use tongs and to place a bevnap over crushed ice while agitating it.

Free-pour vs Jigger-measure: While you may be able to snap a perfect 30ml measure ten-times-out-of-ten in your home bar, the added pressure and adrenalin that comes with performing to a time limit makes free-pouring a shaky competition proposition at best. Inherent risks aside, it is also highly likely that at least one of the judges will regard free-pouring as an absolute no-no in a competition setting, and will mark you down accordingly. The safe bet on all fronts is to jigger-measure everything.

Taste your drink: You should taste your drink as you make it as a matter of course, so that you know things are going to plan and no ingredients have been left out. This becomes doubly important if you are using juices or syrups supplied by the host venue. Additionally, some judges consider tasting drinks to be a non-negotiable part of the cocktail-making process and will penalise a failure to do so. If you favour strawing your drink, as opposed to dabbing a bar spoon on the back of your hand, make sure you discard the used straw: A surprising number of competitors unthinkingly stick the saliver-y end of the straw straight back in the drink, which if spotted by the

judges, costs them the comp.

Face and hair touching: Everyone has physical mannerisms that surface when nervous or under pressure. This often takes the form of an unconscious touching of the face, or repeatedly running the hands through one's hair. If you are such a person, it is doubly important that you use tongs. Even a judge who is normally fine with the handling of ice will mark you down if you touch your hair before doing so. Ask a friend to film one of your competition performances which will help you spot nervous and potentially unsanitary mannerisms that need to be addressed.

Missed ingredients: A surprising number of competitors serve their drink with one or more ingredients missing—often the base spirit. Lining your ingredients up in the order in which they go into the drink and working through them methodically can help avoid this embarrassing cock-up. But there is no substitute for tasting your drink as you make it. If you taste your drink and realise something is not quite right, take a breath and decide whether you should press on or start again. Going over time will cost you some points. But serving a cocktail that omits the sponsor brand will result in disqualification.

Bottle handling: When holding a bottle—whether it be as you speak about it or simply to pour its contents—make sure the label is orientated towards the audience. Some judges consider this to be general good-bartending form. Others like it because they work for the brand. Journalists will also appreciate this because a clearly visible label makes for better photographs.

AVOIDING MISHAPS AND ACCIDENTS

Inanimate objects are out to kill you: Soda syphons, blow torches, smoke guns, cigarette lighters, and any other piece of kit that functions in 'on' and 'off' states will fail when you need it the most. Whenever practicable, bring a backup, and have a plan ready for those occasions when carrying a spare is not an option. Always fire a 'test spurt' of anything pressurised into the sink before aiming it at your drink. I have never seen CO2 foam work properly the first time at a competition. And on several occasions I have witnessed an unexpected rush of foamless gas blow the bulk of a just-poured cocktail out of its glass. In fact, approach anything gas-powered with caution at a cocktail competition.

Beware the Parisian Shaker: By referring to absolutely no carefully-harvested research data—and relying instead on personal experience and anecdotal evidence—I can tell you that at a cocktail competition, there is exactly a 1:3 chance of your Parisian shaker freezing shut. The device looks pretty and is 'on trend' at the moment. But competitions are fraught with potential fuckups, so it makes sense to avoid unnecessary obstacles. If you insist on using a Parisian shaker, make sure you have a never-fails method of opening it should it freeze solid.

Bring more that you need of everything: If you pre-measure your ingredients into little flasks or test tubes, don't leave the bottles at home. Any number of things can happen that will require you to scrap a drink mid-way and start again from scratch. If you have used your only measure of home-made aardvark syrup, you will find yourself screwed. Similarly, beautifully intricate, pre-made garnishes have a tendency to fall into the ice well and disintegrate.

So if you need two, bring four, just in case.

Pre-visualisation prevents spillage: It is entirely possible (although highly inadvisable) that in the lead up to a competition, you will never actually serve your drink to another person. Meaning that up until competition day, you have always made it, gazed lovingly at it for a moment, then necked it. That this is the case for a competitor becomes evident when the person carefully assembles the drink, glassware filled to the rim and finicky garnish is balanced precariously on top, only to have it fall apart and spill everywhere when an attempt is made to serve it to the judges. Visualise yourself serving the drink during the planning stage to prevent such catastrophes. In general, wash lines well shy of the rim are preferable to spilling a drink upon service. Plus, if your garnish can't support its own weight, quit competitions and get a job at Nightjar.

BAR CRAFT AS PERFORMANCE

The previous tips fall under the heading of 'good practice', employing them should ensure you score perfect marks on the 'bar skills' category of the judging sheet. However, certain bar craft techniques go beyond good practice and can be used as an integral part of your presentation. As ever, there are pitfalls to be avoided and I must stress that the advice given below relates to potential problems associated with cocktail competition use only, it is not a judgment on these practices when used 'in the wild'.

Throw with caution: Throwing drinks takes skill and confidence, especially when under competition pressure. The potential for things to go wrong is large and should the cocktail be aflame, there is more at stake than points. Obviously, practice is required. You should be absolutely certain that you can pull the technique off before using it at a competition. It is also important to examine your reasons for throwing a drink. In my humble, judge's opinion, if your drink needs to be properly cold in order to taste good, you should not throw it. If your decision to throw your entry is purely aesthetic, carefully weigh the odds of it tasting good and you not covering yourself and the judges in burning brandy against the extra points you think throwing might bring your presentation score.

Flair-ish?: At some point during the last ten years, flair became uncool, which is a shame because it is fun and everyone secretly enjoys watching it. Even more lamentable than the loss of something which at its heart was quite joyful, is what has arisen in its place—a weird, over-elaborate manner of handing bottles and tools that makes me want to bang my forehead on the bar when I see it used at competitions. There is a fine line between graceful, flowing movement and looking like a twat who has decided to employ three movements despite only one being required. If you want to flair, awesome, go for it. If you want to be smooth, that's great, too. But be aware that many judges will regard middle-ground flouncing as an annoyance, rather than as a beautiful expression of Ichi-go ichi-e. This is totally subjective and quite possibly annoying for some to read, but overly-twirly bottle handling and melodramatic cut-pours are likely to cost you more points than they win. Unless it's a UKBG comp, in which case, there's no such thing as over-elaborate, so knock yourself out.

COMPETITION SHAKES

No, not that 'Japanese Hard Shake' nonsense. By shakes, we mean the hand tremors that afflict every bartender to some degree during their competition career.

At every one of the hundreds of heats I have judged, at least one person has suffered from the shakes, most often in the form of mildly trembling hands that make pouring a measure difficult. In extreme cases, it can cause the hands to shake so violently that using a jigger becomes impossible. On one occasion, a particularly afflicted competitor had to ask the judges to pour his measures for him.

No matter how bad they are, the shakes can add an additional, sometimes unexpected, obstacle to an already stressful situation.

WHAT CAUSES THE SHAKES?

The term you often hear at competitions is 'If you're not rocky, you're too cocky.'

This would imply that the shaky hands which plague some bartenders during competitions have something to do with confidence or mental attitude. This seems to make sense at first glance. But over the years I have seen competitors so nervous they appear to be on the verge of a panic attack perform with rock steady hands. On other occasions, very calm, composed bartenders' hands shake like—to quote Chester's Paul Murphy—'A small dog shitting.'

So, if the shakes are not a result of your state of mind, what causes them? Competition hand tremors are a physiological response to stress. To understand the phenomenon better, I spoke to Consultant Neurologist, Doctor Edward Fathers.

He told us:

'Everybody has a very slight tremor if you hold your hand out in front [of you]; it may be imperceptible but you can't keep your hand completely still, and that is called a physiological tremor. We

all have one to some degree or another. There are many things that can amplify a physiological tremor: states of sleep deprivation, anxiety before an exam, standing up in front of lots of people. It is normal for the tremor to become more marked and of greater amplitude.

The reason for that is adrenalin is the hormone that we produce in states of anxiety, and it is one of the main things that influences the amplitude of a tremor. That's why some people who get very anxious can have a higher degree of tremor. When you have a hangover you are producing more adrenalin, because of the toxins that are swashing round the body, so yes, anything that makes you feel ill will increase your adrenalin levels and amplify the tremor.

There are two things that will regulate, suppress that particular type of tremor. One is a beta blocker, which blocks the receptors that adrenalin works on... GPs will sometimes give that as a symptomatic treatment to get anxious people through interviews and exams, as and when. The other thing that consistently works in 50% of people, if not greater, is alcohol. It is the best drug for suppressing that kind of tremor. You don't normally need much, normally just one or two units will suppress that sort of tremor for an hour or two.'

Perhaps surprisingly then, Dr Fathers' advice is to have a shot about twenty minutes before you are due to perform. You will notice that he doesn't say anything about multiple beers or laybacks. Just a solitary shot to dampen the tremors down. However, as pleasing as this tip is, his comments about hangovers are probably more important.

Leading up to the comp, you will no doubt have asked for the day off to compete, and the temptation to 'just have a couple of drinks' after your shift the night before 'as I don't have to get up early to-morrow' will be strong. My advice to you is don't do it. Go home. Eat some good food. Get a good night's sleep. Wake up refreshed. Have breakfast. Head to the competition venue intact and bushy-tailed.

As obvious as this would seem, lots of people don't do it. They turn up to competitions in the grips of a hangover. In that state, their bodies are already fighting an internal battle to stay upright, and the extra stress-released adrenalin is often enough to give them a debilitating case of the shakes. Getting a good night's kip the night before might not seem very rock 'n' roll. But if there's a big prize on offer and you want to win it, one night of abstinence is a reasonable price to pay.

HOW TO WORK AROUND THE SHAKES

Having said all of that, some bartenders do all the right things, and still get the shakes. If you find yourself prone to them, there are a few simple things you can do to mitigate them:

Stay cool: First and foremost, don't get flustered: The judges and spectators have seen this before and likely experienced it them-selves, so there is no need to feel embarrassed.

Make light of it: If you feel comfortable with an unscripted interaction with the judges, make a joke about your shaky hands. Show them you know what is happening and that you can cope regardless.

Delete the jigger: Pre-measure all of your ingredients into lit-tle bottles or flasks to avoid jiggering. If you do this, make sure you explain what is in each bottle, and how much.

Keep it simple: Avoid finicky garnishes that need to be balanced on the glass rim. Also, think about the glassware you are going to use. If you always get the shakes, wide vessels with a low centre of gravity are a better bet than tall, unstable ones.

Short pour: Wash lines that come slightly shy of the lip of the glass are preferable to spilling half of the drink when you serve it to the judges.

Don't use spoons: Perennial shakers should use an eyedropper for tiny measures, as opposed to the 'fraction of a bar spoon' method.

CHAPTER 8
Types of Judge

FREAKS, GEEKS, AND HACKS

As shocking[1] as this may be to hear, not every cocktail competition judge has a finely tuned palate.

Journalists are invited to judge because they will provide post-event coverage. A regional brand rep will judge because they want to develop a relationship with the area's bartenders. An ambassador will judge so that the brand's values are represented on the panel.

At some competitions it is entirely possible that nobody on the judging panel will know a well-balanced drink should it bite them on the arse. While, of course, on other occasions, you will be asked to perform before a panel of bartender-legends who posses intimidating levels of knowledge and experience. On still other occasions, you will be expecting one set of judges but be confronted by another set entirely, because people sometimes fall ill[2], or public transport lets them down[3].

Such foibles make attempting to tailor your drink or presentation towards a specific judge or judges a waste of time. However, a spot

---

1   Not remotely shocking.
2   Are hungover.
3   They overslept.

of lazy profiling is on order, so that you can recognise some of the types of competition judge and be equipped to deal with them.

THE CLEAN FREAK

Whatever your thoughts on handling ice, this judge wants to see some tong action. He or she will take a dim view of your skin touching anything that ends up in the drink and will deduct points accordingly. Conversely, points will often be added for over-elaborate handling of bottles and showy pours. The Clean Freak can often be identified by a slightly-too-tight white shirt and arm garters (although the person may have dressed down for the comp and be sporting a UKBG t-shirt instead). As a rough and prescriptive rule of thumb, if you are being judged by someone with a hotel background, your cleanliness and bar craft will be under the microscope.

THE SPIRITS GEEK

The Spirits Geek will take copious notes and ask to taste anything home-made you include in your drink. Have plenty of straws to hand and be prepared for your carefully planned presentation to be derailed by questions. This person knows (or thinks he or she know) more than you about, well, everything booze-related. So your product knowledge needs to be up to scratch. Often recognisable by their desire to talk about cold-brew coffee, the Spirits Geek thinks of cocktail competitions as interactive events. So be prepared to answer questions and explain your choice of ingredients.

THE HUNGOVER LOCAL HERO

This well-loved and much-respected individual has been in the game for years and trained most of the young bartenders in town. The trouble is, the person hasn't been able to taste anything since 2007, when on a brand trip to Mexico, he or she drank some new-make Tequila straight off the still, which cauterised every taste bud. In addition to this judging handicap, the person also had a big night last night, and thus needs plenty of water to sip plus lively, entertaining chat to take his or her mind off the hangover. Should you be competing towards the end of the field and notice this individual get a second wind, consider offering them a shot before you kick off.

THE ONE WITH THE CHIP IN THEIR HEAD

When this judge started working for the sponsor brand's marketing department, a small microchip was implanted in the person's cerebral cortex which overrides all naturally occurring thoughts and feelings. The person will wear a shiny suit and quite possibly still own a Blackberry, which is constantly checked. While this judge's senses of taste and smell are modulated by the brain chip, but he or she does respond well to branding and sales figures. If you encounter one, be sure to point out that your entry has been listed on your bar's menu and is a top seller. At some stage, late in the evening, this judge will ask you if you 'know anybody who delivers'. At this point, call a cab and send the person back to the home charging pod.

LOCAL PRESS HACKS AND LIFESTYLE BLOGGERS

You're pretty much screwed. Nothing you say or serve will make much of an impression. However providing such judges with plenty of opportunities to take nice photos for Instagram and Facebook will garner points: So will the implication that free drinks await, should he or she visit your bar which will never happen because by the time the competition ends, the person will be too drunk to remember anything you or anyone else said.

THE WEARY TRADE JOURNALIST

If it's someone from BarLifeUK, just show him or her a purchase receipt for this book and you're golden. If it's anyone else, make an effort to say your name and the name of your drink clearly. Offer to write down both details if you get the impression the journo hasn't got it. As the competition progresses, the person's handwriting will deteriorate to the point it becomes illegible. The next day, it's odds-on that your carefully recorded details will be the only part of their notes the person can read, meaning you'll get a mention in the article, win or lose.

CHAPTER 9
Dress Code

ABSOLUTELY NO WIFE-BEATERS

A few years ago, back in the days when Tiki competitions hovered somewhere between fun and dangerous, I judged a bartender who was wearing a wife-beater. His choice of shirt hadn't really registered with me until he reached across the bar to serve his drink, and I saw a bead of sweat, about the size of a match head, drip from his armpit hair and into the ice well. From that moment onward, I have taken a dim view of sleeveless shirts behind the bar in general and as competition apparel in particular.

Tiki competitions and their requisite hula shirts aside, the wider subject of what to wear while competing bears a little thought. We have witnessed a change in what is acceptable and what isn't over the last ten years, driven primarily by the rise of social media. As proudly nonconformist as the bar industry is, the fact that photographs of cocktail competitions will appear on official brand Facebook and Instagram feeds means that 'inappropriate' attire will harm your chances of winning.

Inappropriate does not necessarily mean revealing or somehow unfashionable. It refers to what is printed on your clothing: In other words, turn up to a Mount Gay comp wearing a Wray & Nephew t-shirt and the sponsor brand will be reluctant to declare you the winner because they don't want photos of Uncle Wray's logo on their Facebook feed. The same goes for shirts emblazoned with any word or image that could be described as 'not safe for work'.

Rude words and competitor branding aside, you probably can't go too far wrong by dressing for the venue in which the competition will take place, in which case, a Martini comp held at the Beaufort Bar requires a different outfit to a Mai Tai comp at Trailer Happiness.

As usual, the big global competitions differ slightly, in so much as they require competitors to be dressed like hotel bartenders at all times regardless of the competition venue. For male competitors, this appears to demand the wearing of shirts and suit trousers that are one size too small and incredibly uncomfortable-looking. But with luck that will change as time goes on.

In truth, I died a little inside while writing this section, because you should be able to dress however the fuck you want. If you find yourself being judged at a competition by BarLifeUK, rest assured we won't mark you down for wearing the wrong t-shirt, although others might. Wife-beaters are still verboten, however.

ACTION POINTS

- Dress for the competition venue
- Avoid competitor-branded and NSFW t-shirts
- Absolutely no wife-beaters

CHAPTER 10
Learning From Feedback

MAKE EVERY HEAT COUNT

Some bartenders view competitions as part of their career development path. They have a clearly defined objective, which could be securing investment in order to open their own joint or becoming a global brand ambassador. They enter competitions strategically, picking only those they feel will help them achieve that goal.

Other bartenders take a more ad-hoc approach, entering the occasional competition because they have a fondness for the sponsor brand or they find themselves particularly attracted to its prize.

Either approach is perfectly valid, although it is perhaps easier for the bartender with a plan who is regularly competing to improve, as practice does make perfect.

In either case, it makes sense to treat your competition career as a cumulative effort, during which each competition entered adds to a store of knowledge that will help improve future performances. All this approach requires is a notepad, and a little self discipline.

GET AS MUCH FEEDBACK AS POSSIBLE

Win or lose, the moment a competition result is announced the temptation will be to relax, neck a beer, and get on with the rest of the night. However, before the competition breaks up and organisers and judges drift off to other bars or go home, you should ask for feedback.

If possible, get feedback from each judge on the panel, someone from the brand, and any friends or colleagues who came to support you. Write down what they say, stick the notepad somewhere safe, and then get on with the serious business of celebrating, drowning a loser's sorrows, or trying to pull that bartender with all the tattoos who travelled in from a small town for his or her first comp, as appropriate.

TURN FEEDBACK INTO A PLAN OF ACTION

Typing that subheading made me a little sick in my mouth, because it seems like something a junior advertising executive would be told during a yearly appraisal. However, as corporate as it might sound, doing so will help you win more comps than just about anything else. This is the case because while bartenders often ask judges for feedback after competitions, seldom is the process of working the advice formalised into the next attempt. In the months between competitions, the sting of being beaten, which caused the bartender to ask for feedback in the first place, fades, and so does the memory of what the judges said. At best it becomes a vague mental note to 'spend less time talking about pirates and more time talking about aardvarks'. At worst, it is forgotten altogether and the bartender makes the same mistakes at the next competition.

To avoid this—in the days following a competition—spend some time dissecting the feedback you were given. Look for common themes: If the same fault is pointed out by multiple observers, you know it is something that needs attention. In a similar vein, if several people were particularly impressed with a facet of your drink or presentation, you can safely use it again, perhaps even building your next entry around it. In this way, positive feedback is just as important as constructive, negative feedback.

At the end of this process, your objective should be to have several defined things to work on next time. Applying fixes to identified problems and capitalising on things you got right, becomes as important as understanding and adhering to the rules of the next competition you enter.

CREATE A COMPETITION BLACK BOOK

If we break the competition process down into its constituent parts, we get something along the lines of this: Understand the brief and conduct initial research; develop a drink and presentation; compete; learn lessons from feedback.

Your thought processes—mistakes and successes from each of these four stages—should be recorded. In this instance, an old-fashioned, Moleskine-style paper notebook works best. If you imagine a section of the notebook devoted to a particular competition, the last things you record would be the 'identified things to focus on' mentioned in the previous paragraph.

However, these should be written in the first page on the next competition's section, not the last page of the previous one. In this way, even if months pass between competitions, the next time you begin the process of developing an entry, the first things you see in your journal will be the lessons you learned the last time you competed.

As your competition career develops, this journal will fill with personal, tailored learning and experience to which you can always refer. Having such a resource means you will never have to start working on a competition from a blank page; you will always have the things you learned last time there in front of you as a place to start. It also means there is no such thing as a bad result. Viewed through the lens of a competition career built of cumulative learning, any losses, even bad ones, are just another step along the way. Recording and learning from each heat makes losses just as valuable as wins, and the only wasted heat becomes the one you learned nothing from.

ACTION POINTS

•   Get as much feedback as possible from judges and organisers, and ask a friend to video your performance
•   Record this feedback, and boil it down to defined things to work on next time
•   Start your next comp with what you learned at the last comp
•   Consider starting a competition journal or Black Book.

PART THREE

- **Advice for Judges**
- **Advice for Competition Organisers**
- **Competition Journal Template**

CHAPTER 11
Advice for Competition Judges

Bartenders and brand folk asked to judge cocktail competitions for the first time are rarely told how to do it well. Given that competition results and the way they are delivered can effect the career development and emotional wellbeing of fellow human beings, it is something that should be done right.

With that in mind, the duties of a good competition judge break down into three main areas of responsibility: Take it seriously; Be consistent; Don't be a dick.

Take it Seriously

At first glance, cocktail competitions appear to be convivial affairs. Quite often sponsor brand or PR staff will be on hand, excited to find themselves in a bar instead of the office, and eager to make everyone feel welcome. There will also be people who haven't seen each other for a while, enthusiastically catching up on old times, and of course, that one bartender who thinks saying 'boom' and 'fuck yeah' a lot will disguise the fact they are still drunk from last night and about to pass out. As a judge, you will probably be given nice things to eat and drink, and told to relax while someone wrangles the competitors. Good times.

However, in addition to the fun and frolics, you are also guaranteed to find someone in the bar who has poured their heart and soul into their entry, and desperately wants to win. Someone else will have spent their last £10 on a train ticket to the venue. And one of the other people is so nervous, they may well vomit into the ice well.

Competitors invest time, effort, money, and emotional energy into competitions. So while enjoyment of the judging experience is to be encouraged, always remember why you are there.

Write notes alongside your category scores: As the competition progresses and your understanding of the standard of the field develops, it may become necessary to go back to early competitors and revise their scores. This is much easier to do if you have written down brief explanations of your marks. This also helps you deliver useful feedback after the competition.

Be prepared to give feedback: You will be asked for feedback, usually by bartenders who lost and want to know how they can improve. If the heat you judged was a qualifier, the winner might ask if you noticed any flaws that can be corrected in time for the final. And, on vary rare occasions, you may find yourself face-to-face with an angry bartender who disagrees with the result. In all cases, correctly filled out judging sheets with explanatory notes next to the scores are your friend. The BarLifeUK method is to sit down and go through our sheets with competitors who ask for feedback, explaining our rationale for each category mark and overall impressions, so we fill our sheets out in a manner that means they can be shown to competitors. This is vastly superior to blushing as you give a vague explanation for the three-out-of-ten mark you awarded two hours ago—from memory—to a bartender who thinks he or she should have won the comp.

Understand the category criteria: Before the comp begins, make sure you understand the scoring categories properly. This may seem self evident, but sometimes brands use labels like 'presentation', which could mean the appearance of the drink, or chat, which can lead to confusion. Also, views on categories such as 'replicability' and 'originality' can vary wildly from person to person. So such nebulous subjects are worth discussing with the other judges and the sponsor to settle on proper definitions.

BE CONSISTENT

Most people don't mind being beaten in any sort of competition, as long as the playing field is level. On the rare occasions BarLifeUK have encountered disgruntled competitors, the point of argument has invariably been the interpretation of a rule, or a flexing of the rules afforded to one competitor, but not the others. In each case, the problem was caused by a lack of consistency among the judges.

Clarify time limits and penalties: It is human nature to give a competitor the benefit of the doubt if the person goes over time by a couple of seconds. But how about ten seconds, or twenty? As long as the same 'grace period' is applied to everyone, it doesn't matter how long it is. The judges need to agree to this before the competition starts and communicate it to the bartenders.

Remember your time warnings: If the judges or organiser tell the competitors they will get a warning at the 'sixty seconds remaining' point, make sure it happens. If someone didn't get a promised time check and then goes overtime, the judges don't have a leg to stand on if complaints are made.

Clarify what home-made means: This one crops up all

the time. Most competition briefs limit the number of home-made ingredients that are allowed in an entry drink. If a bartender says 'I made this aardvark syrup myself, but you could use the Monin version', does that count towards the home-made tally? Again, it doesn't matter what the answer is, as long as it is the same for everyone.

Think twice about accepting shots from competitors: This tends to happen more frequently at rum and Tequila comps. While fun, picture it from the perspective of the last competitor, taking a turn behind the stick having watched the panel get slowly hammered and lose all sense of taste.

DON'T BE A DICK

This breaks down into two parts: Intentional dickishness, and unintentional dickishness. The intentional variety involves forgetting competitors have feelings and channelling Simon Cowell. The unintentional kind is generally the result of not paying enough attention. Both are to be avoided.

Considerate questioning: Sometimes sponsors will brief judges to ask questions of each competitor. On other occasions, judges feel the need to ask questions of their own accord. In either case, timing is everything: interrupting a bartender mid-flow can completely ruin the train of thought and derail the whole presentation. It's much better to wait for a natural pause. Questions should also be asked in a conversational tone and with a smile. You are not Frost and the bartender is not Nixon.

Poker face: If a competitor is flustered, nervous, or otherwise struggling, the last thing the person needs is to see is the judges rolling their eyes at each other.

Pay attention: If you feel it is acceptable look at your phone while the competitor is doing his or her best to communicate, it is likely your level of dickishness is beyond the reach of this book. You should stop reading this now.

CHAPTER 12
Advice for Competition Organisers

Whether it be a small, local heat or a huge global affair, at a fundamental level, all cocktail competitions share the same success criteria:

- Lots of bartenders enter
- Everyone turns up on the day, the competition runs smoothly, and a worthy winner is selected
- The competition successfully engages with the trade

With these points in mind, here are some things we have learned over the past ten years of running competitions, and working with sponsor brands as media partner.

GENERATING ENTRIES

Complexity of concept is inversely proportionate to the number of entries received: Competitions are expensive. For smaller brands, competitions can often represent the biggest marketing investment they make in a year. As such, there is a temptation to over-engineer the concept in an effort to tick the 'trade marketing', 'consumer marketing', and 'keeping the brand owners happy' boxes all at once. While this is possible to do, executed poorly it can severely limit the number of entries the competition will receive.

For example, consumer marketing will often employ nebulous campaigns designed to look good on TV and appeal to vague consumer aspirations (think Christmas perfume commercials). A drinks brand that tries to tie a competition to such a consumer campaign by saying 'Conjure the spirit of a hot wind blowing through the exotic streets of Marrakesh with your cocktail and presentation' is going to get far fewer entries than one that says 'Create a summer cocktail'.

That's not to say there is anything wrong with conceptual competitions, just that if entry numbers are a key concern, a simpler format is the way to go.

The complexity of an entry mechanism is inversely proportionate to the number of entries generated: A simple web entry form which asks for contact details, recipe spec, and supporting statement delivers the best results. Requesting a photograph of the drink causes a drop-off in entries. Stipulating a video must be filmed is more-or-less the death nell for a competition. We cannot say for sure why this is. But a rise in the required effort-level probably has something to do with it, as does the fact that while everyone has a smartphone these days, not everyone feels confident to shoot decent photographs and video footage.

The quality of the prize is directly proportionate to the number of entries generated: Competition prizes that include a trip to Tales of the Cocktail or some overseas distillery have become ubiquitous because they work very well as an entry incentive. However, not every brand has this level of budget to play with, and in such cases, we have found that even modest cash prizes work very well. Competitions which offer around £500-£1000 to the winner generally receive a similar number of entries as competitions with travel-based prizes.

At the other end of the spectrum, brand-organised competitions that advertise 'a bottle of booze and the kudos of winning' as their prize can invariably be seen posting 'Hooray, the deadline to our competition has been extended' status updates on Facebook. Which, as everybody knows, is a sign that no-one has entered, and that the competition will be quietly cancelled.

ON THE DAY

Minimising No-Shows: It's incredibly frustrating when previously confirmed competitors fail to show up to competitions, primarily because their place could have been given to someone else. Sending an email to the competitors three days before the heat provides a memory-jog. Should there be drop-outs, this also leaves enough time to fill any gaps in the lineup. It is also important that someone at the heat has the competitor's phone numbers, so that latecomers can be tracked down. Both of these measures seem obvious, but are often forgotten or overlooked.

Food, Food, Food, Food: Cocktail competitions involve lots of waiting around in the proximity of free alcoholic drinks. Organisers who wish their competitors to remain upright and functional for the duration of the comp should provide them with food.

Competitor Numbers: In our experience, the ideal number of competitors to invite to a heat is twelve. Should a couple drop out, that still leaves enough for a respectable field. Should they all turn up, twelve remains a manageable number. Bear in mind that a heat which accommodates more than about fifteen bartenders is going to run for the best part of a day, which is a long time to ask a group of bartenders to loiter and a lot of drinks for the judges to assess. In such cases, it is better to paper judge the entries down to a tight field of the best twelve entries or run two heats.

TRADE ENGAGEMENT

Prize Coverage: If your brand is running a competition with a travel-based prize, a travelogue-type story which follows the winner along the journey makes for a powerful entry recruitment tool should you run the competition again. If it proves impossible to send a trade media journalist on the trip, ask the winner to write it, providing assistance as needed. Most trade media outlets will be open to content submissions of this kind, especially if they are free. And most bartenders will be happy for the chance to be published.

Co-ordinate with Reps and Ambassadors: This is another one of those things that seems obvious, but is often missed. Once a cocktail competition is announced, the sponsor brand's reps should promote it within bars and support anyone who wants to enter with training and brand knowledge. The lead up to a comp is also the perfect time for brand ambassadors to schedule masterclass sessions that will both support and encourage entries. This kind of face-to-face contact in the weeks before a competition also dramatically minimises the chance of unannounced no-shows on the day.

Consider Covering Travel Costs: It is not always possible to hold a multitude of heats throughout the country, primarily for budgetary reasons. While most bartenders understand this and are willing to travel large distances to attend a competition with a single regional heat, not all are able to afford it. Once the competition entry deadline has passed and paper judging is complete, brands who go on to contribute towards the travel costs of competitors from out of town garner a lot of good will within the bartending community, and find word of mouth on their side when it comes to recruiting for future competitions.

CHAPTER 13
Copmetition Journal Template

Competition Name	Sponsor Brand

Summary of Competition Brief

Competition Rules

Feedback Action Points from Last Comp

Initial Ideas

Recipe Theme

Presentation Theme

Recipe Version One

Tasting Notes and Potential Improvements

Recipe Final Spec

Brand Knowledge Key Points

Presentation Outline

Performance Timing

Competition Day Checklist

Sufficient ice in well

All needed tools easily to hand

Glassware in chiller

All ingredients present and lined up in the correct order

Garnish present

Request a one minute warning from the judges

Breath, compose yourself

Knock them dead

Feedback from Judges

Afterward

'The worst place to experience an urgent need to urinate is the back seat of a helicopter, as it flies over a glacier in New Zealand.'

'Russian police officers don't like to be asked the way to the nearest kebab shop by drunk Englishmen at 3 o'clock in the morning.'

These weird observations, and many others, are mine to make thanks to cocktail competitions. Being involved with comps has allowed me to meet wonderful people and do extraordinary things in parts of the world I would have otherwise never visited, and I can honestly say that two of the best days of my life were spent during global competition finals.

If you are a bartender contemplating a competition career, I urge you to get stuck in because a week away with a group of your peers, on a brand's dime, is something you should experience at least once. Don't allow a few disappointing results to put you off, that's just part of the process. Stick with it, apply feedback and learn from your mistakes, and you will soon find yourself drinking a 5am Guinness at an airport Wetherspoons.

Of course, there is more to a competition than its prize - at their heart, comps are concerned with learning. This 'new golden age of cocktails' that we inhabit has come about in large part because bartenders know more about spirits now than ever before. A ten-year period of back-to-back cocktail competitions can claim some responsibility for this development. Every competition entry sees a new drink added to the lexicon of modern cocktails, and each nugget of information learned adds to a store of bartending lore that can be shared and passed on. In no small way, cocktail competitions, their sponsor brands, and the bartenders who enter them, have forged a link between the world's cocktail cities, and transformed the industry into a relentlessly creative, global community. Which is not bad, considering the cocktail competition started out in life as nothing more that an excuse for bartenders to get drunk, wear hula shirts, and light shit on fire.

I hope reading this book has helped equip and inspire you to enter the next cocktail competition that catches your eye. If so, good luck, and I might see you there,

About the Author

Andy Ives' drinks-writing career began in the late 1990s, working for *The Publican Newspaper* and its cocktail magazine spinoff, *Flavour*. He later joined *CLASS*, as editor of the magazine's first website, before moving to Australia to become editor of *Industry Magazine* (cocktail bar design and interiors), and bars editor of *Australian Bartender Magazine*.

In 2009, Andy partnered with Simon Webster to launch bar industry website BarLifeUK. The site flourished, and BarLifeUK is now the first place bartenders look for cocktail competition news, entries, and results. Andy remains BarLifeUK's editor, and an active competition judge.

Lightning Source UK Ltd.
Milton Keynes UK
UKOW01f0926280717
306236UK00001B/170/P

9 781907 434501